THE MAKING BONES

SERIES BOOK 1

THE STREET HUSTLER'S GUIDEBOOK

A "Syndicated" Guide To Corporate Mobility and Promotion

WRITTEN BY MOJO

MONKEY BUSINESS PUBLISHING • NORTH CAROLINA

ISBN: 979-8723871977

Publisher: Monkey Business Publishing

For my soldiers, legitimate and otherwise. Thank you for your respect and your hard work. You are my wolfpack.

~ Mojo

Contents

INTRODUCTION

Introduction

Getting ahead and staying ahead has long been a concern in both criminal and legitimate business enterprises. In pursuit of this, ambitious individuals have always sought knowledge from the achievements of those successful individuals before them. There exist a great many books for individuals navigating their ambitions through legitimate business armed with education, opportunity, wealth, or family pedigree. This book is not for those individuals.

This book assumes you are not starting with education, opportunity, wealth, and/or pedigree. This book assumes you came up hustling in the streets like I did. At 8 years old I was hustling candy at school. 10 years old I was hustling groceries to shut-ins and retirees. By 13, I was brokering protection and selling cigarettes to my fellow middle schoolers. I hustled so hard that I once got busted working as a parking lot attendant collecting parking fees from the people who owned the parking lot. I collected a pocket full of money from people that paid me just based on my confidence. They were members of the organization that owned the land but blindly gave their money over to a teenager in a vest because they didn't know any better. If only I had been able to outrun that fat cop.

However, I wasn't a stereotypical, delinquent street kid. I was fixing and selling bicycles with stolen parts to help my parents keep the heat on and buy groceries. My younger criminal activity was about food and utilities. However, I never had much serious trouble with the law. I never got in trouble at school. I did plenty of bad shit, but I was pretty good at staying below the radar. I was gifted in school and got top grades. I actually turned down a college scholarship because my family needed me to be working. In my world, college was a luxury for spoiled rich kids. I was born a hustler. There is no B.S. in Hustle (pun intended). Does any of this sound familiar? If you came from nothing (or less than nothing like me), you can still make opportunities for yourself. You can hustle your way up. To pursue ambition as a street kid, you must be more intelligent, cunning, and tenacious than your privileged competition. *Your* ambition requires that you be a ruthless fucking hustler.

Your ambition also requires wisdom. However, where can people like us find wisdom? There are thousands of books written by successful people who found success through education and investment. Where are the books about street kids turned C.E.O.? Most street kids end up dead, in prison, or the worst - grinding out a living in a menial job with their name on their shirt after they have the ambition forcibly squeezed out of them through years of monotony.

It doesn't have to end that way. You just need a practical example. You need to study a successful organization that holds the value of work ethic above education. You need to study an organization that doesn't follow the same path that all those other thousands of books describe. You need to study how to turn common sense and human nature into a capital enterprise. Your success requires that you pull wisdom from the most successful international wealth-generating organization in history built, almost exclusively, by people without formal education, opportunity, wealth, or pedigree. You need an organization made up of opportunistic, ambitious, self-motivated street hustlers like us. You need the long-concealed wisdom of La Cosa Nostra, the Mob, the Mafia, the Syndicate, the Outfit (as I called it). You need to stop thinking like a street dog and start thinking like a wolf.

A pack of street dogs usually has a leader. The leader is usually very selfish and is frequently challenged. Every day, the pack scavenges for what they need, and any time one dog finds a scrap, they whole pack fights each other to get a piece until it is gone and they all return to scavenging. All the dogs in the pack are scarred and malnourished. They just drift around scrapping with each other and having no clear discernable path or goal. They survive.

A pack of wolves has clear, rarely challenged leadership. Wolves find, stalk, and kill prey. They outthink the prey, trap it, then through perfectly choreographed procedures, each wolf does their part and they are able to kill prey multiple times their size. The lead wolf sees that the youngest and the females are looked after before the soldiers. He does this because he knows the soldiers will keep hunting until they are fed. By using that to his advantage, the lead wolf knows when the soldiers stop hunting, everyone is nourished. They wake with the sun each day on a clear mission. They have a goal and the pack is single-minded in the pursuit of it. They thrive

Like the wolf, you need to know how to show respect, follow when required, seize your opportunities, and hustle your way up through the pack. If you study dogs, you learn to fight. If you study wolves, you learn to hunt. *The Street Hustler's Guidebook* will provide an adaptation of the wisdom of the Outfit without the brutality. Using the wisdom in this book, you will find a place in the system where you will be rewarded inordinately. Welcome to the pack, keep up, do what you're told, and don't get bit.

These lessons will apply in both legitimate business and otherwise but, I am strongly encouraging you to use this wisdom legitimately. The lessons can bring you success in both worlds but "retirement" in legitimate business is much more enjoyable. Retirement from "otherwise" businesses is usually involuntary. Besides that, my former colleagues do not want to be overrun by wanna-be wise guys screwing up their profit margins and harassing their customers and clients. They react poorly to competition. Stay out of their world. You've been warned.

The Street Hustler's Guidebook will guide you through nine chapters of need-to-know information if you intend to give up the name-on-your-shirt hourly job and chase your ambitions like a wolf. I will discuss how you get to know who to know and how to get them to give you an opportunity. I will cover preparing for an "interview" and how to leave that interview with the job you want. Once you start, you will need to know the beginner's rules that nobody else will tell you, but you can find in the following pages. I will go over how to make people trust and use you while allowing you to use them by selecting and building a relationship with an appropriate mentor. I will cover basic business principles but I will give you the real truth behind each of them so you can protect yourself and work toward advancement without tripping over unrealistic academic definitions. In order to complete your assigned undertakings, you need to know what can and cannot be done, and you need to know what you will earn in exchange. To help you be successful in your new job, I'm going to go over time management and decision making. These two skills will be critical to advancing yourself past your entry level position. Using the skills you learn from *The Street Hustler's Guidebook,* you will undoubtedly find success in your assignments. In return for your stewardship of their trust, you will receive the confidence and consideration of those above you with greater power. Before long, you will need to know how to navigate office politics and remain unscathed by jealous coworkers and insecure colleagues. And finally, through all of this journey, you will build relationships. Some will be good, some will be bad, and some will be hard to distinguish. The book will finish up with some advice about managing those relationships to optimize your opportunities to advance to the next level. Every person who has successfully risen to the top in the ferocious world of business did so because they are proficient in the art of managing others, both above and below their position in the organization. Just because you are new, does not mean you won't be managing people. The leadership and management in this book are about getting you mobile on the corporate ladder, and demonstrating your proficiency as a beginner will be rocket fuel for your career.

The Street Hustler's Guidebook will throw out the conventional and invariably flawed wisdom of academia in favor of the knowledge and precepts of the ruthless street bosses that built the largest, most profitable, and long-lived organizations in history. Men whose wisdom, despite being based entirely on profitability and growth, is now, unfortunately, remembered for the brutal barbarism of the common, unsophisticated gangster. *The Street Hustler's Guidebook* will look past the brutality and bad press to uncover the pure capitalist ingenuity, fortitude, and seldom seen understanding of human nature which built the Outfit. In doing so this book will provide a guide to success for all people who lack education, opportunity, wealth, or family pedigree. *The Street Hustler's Guidebook* is a guidebook for street kids, mutts, and hustlers like me.

I have built a career by unsavory and unscrupulous means that I won't detail here. However, as I advanced through the same methods I'm sharing with you, I had a mentor who helped me transition into legitimate business. Once I left the Outfit, I found that many of the things which benefited me in their world still benefit me in my legitimate enterprises. I'm still not entirely legitimate and I make my payments every month for my right to operate my legitimate enterprises. However, I used the principles in *The Street Soldier's Guidebook* to climb the ladder, build my wealth and reputation, and negotiate my right to retire legitimate-ish. My hope for you, young hustler, is that you can skip the unsavory and unscrupulous means and go straight to legitimate success and advancement.

CHAPTER 1
Bulding Your Reputation

Building Your Reputation

To enter the Outfit, you have to be sponsored. If you are born into it, your father sponsors you for membership. Otherwise, you must have a reputation on the street or in the joint. That reputation has to include proper respect, intelligence, cunning, and tenacity. On top of all that, you must be a proven hard ass. There are methods you use to build that reputation. You never brag but you make sure anything impressive you do will have an audience with at least one bigmouth in attendance. If you fight, you fight the biggest guy and you make an example of him. You ensure that his swollen eyes spread your reputation for weeks. Nobody needs to know you slipped something in his drink beforehand and weighted your fist with a roll of quarters during the fight. You arrange circumstances which allow you to do a favor for someone important. You cut the valve stem on the car of the local caporegime's wife, then follow her so you can play hero and change the tire out for her "no charge". You find

---

and deliver valuable information to sources which are willing to connect you to your opportunity. You know where there is a gate with a loose lock, no cameras, and a sleepy security guard that leads to a storage unit full of DVD players. Why wouldn't you trade that information for a lunch meeting with the capo. Why would he refuse when he already remembers hearing your name from his wife as the nice boy that changed out her tire? You do these things repeatedly until you convert everyone who knows you into a mouthpiece repeating your name and rep until it falls across the ear of opportunity.

In legitimate business, they call this pursuit of opportunity networking. I'll bet you thought networking meant shaking hands, passing out business cards, and emailing your resume into everyone's spam folder twice a month. You would be wrong. Effective networking is a legitimate form of the manipulation above. If you want to make opportunities instead of waiting for them, you need to master active, aggressive networking.

While I am not advocating larceny, assault, or damage to personal property, I am encouraging you to rethink the methods you use to network. Networking is not a passive activity. It is not a "lunch-and-learn" at the local chamber of commerce. It is not chatting with people you met in a Facebook group at 2am. Be proactive and steal your opportunity. Leave the fucking house and go meet people. Meet real people because the Facebook friend that said they were getting you an interview doesn't even work there. If they did, they wouldn't be on Facebook at 2am because they would have a job to wake up for. They're either a hopeless loser, a middle-schooler making you the joke of all his friends, or a douchebag multi-level marketer waiting for the right time to tell you how to make money, "selling products people already buy" while you wait for the interview they aren't getting you. Put that nonsense out of your mind and let's look at what real networking means in the legitimate business world.

Get Face to Face

These days, all you damn kids want to do is on a computer
screen. Like it or not, networking is establishing personal
interactions. Get off your ass, out of your parents' basement,
and go shake hands with someone you admire. I grew up
stealing food and selling cigarettes and I still knew more
about respect than most overprivileged, entitled, and
spineless kids today. Emailing somebody that works where
you want to work is not going to make you stand out. With
that approach, you deserve to be sent to the spam folder and
ignored. Attend events, parties, and gatherings. If you're a
cry-baby and can't go by yourself, find someone in your
network to attend with you. Maybe they can hold your hand
or wipe your mouth for you. Regardless, it doesn't matter if
it's a convention or job fair or your own family holiday
dinner. If you can meet people from outside your current
network with shared interests, you need to be there meeting
as many new faces as possible and exchanging names and

handshakes. Be sure to mention to those you speak with that you are searching for an opportunity and be able to explain what opportunity you are looking for. Practice turning conversation topics toward the job you want. Anybody you meet that shows special promise toward helping you, take them to lunch, get it?

Pick a target. The saying isn't, "ready, fire, aim." You need a target to direct your efforts toward. You can pick multiple targets but "firing" with no target is a losing plan. Find a person you want to be. Find someone you can respect and learn from. Find your "capo" and work your way through their door. Be respectful but persistent and get through that door. You also need to be expanding your network during this time. Don't focus on just one way through the door. Work every possible angle. You want your name mentioned to your target by their family, their friends, their priest, their lawyer, and their barista. Anybody that tries to stop you walking through your target's door is your next networking opportunity. Security guards, secretaries, assistants, even the janitor if they stand between you and what you want. Make every barrier your ally until you can walk in the front door and straight to the office you want to be in, never passing an unfriendly face. Easier said than done, right? Nope, it's only **five principles** applied over and over and over again.

Principle 1: Offer Help

Networking is about turning outward and collecting favors. Whether you are speaking to an ally or an obstacle your networking conversations need to be based around favors. Your goal is to help them, not for them to help you. You just need to initiate a friendly and informal conversation with the first person in the network that will get you where you want to be. Talk about weather, shoes, jewelry, cars, or anything else you can get them to talk about. Once they start talking, all you have to do is keep them talking and listen. Most people enjoy talking when they can do it uninterrupted. So, don't interrupt. Listen to everything and find an opportunity to help them. They won't always offer you an opportunity or ask for help but if you listen well, you will find opportunities to help them. If they are having a party, offer a recipe, offer a discount through a connection, or offer to dress up like a big purple fucking dinosaur if that is what they need, and it gets you started on your network. Don't act like a desperate stooge but you need to endear yourself to them.

Now, you don't need to make a habit of dressing as cartoon characters for spoiled kids. As your network grows and you get closer and closer to your target, you need to reign in the types of favors you are doing. Start listening for opportunities to help that will allow you to display your *relative* skills. Don't mow the grass unless you're trying to be a landscaper. Listen for big projects, stressful events, labor shortages or anything at the place of business where you want to end up. If your connection says he's working the weekend to do some prep work on a big project, take him coffee in the morning and beg to help him prepare. Respect any confidential information but find anything you can do to help, figure out how to convince them to trust you with it. Come back at lunch time to take lunch orders and deliver the orders. Think of the little things that your connection hasn't thought of yet and help resolve them.

Every bit of help you can deliver to your contacts and connections improves your chances of getting the opportunity you are pursuing. Every favor you do gets you closer to your target. Endear yourself to them so they want you to succeed. The big picture here is to do for others so they feel obligated to do for you.

Remember that offering help is about taking action. It is about driving forward and starting to make your bones. Don't talk about it, be about it. Volunteering to help your connections can illustrate your motivation and dedication. It also shows your potential and work ethic. As long as you don't screw the whole damn thing up, you can't go wrong when you do favors for people in a position to advance you toward your goals. Just be careful to never overextend

yourself and never promise anything you can't deliver.

Principle 2: Fight Your Fear

Weakness is not a virtue. You don't have to magically stop

being an introvert. I understand that you cannot just flip a

switch and turn your nerves off. However, you need to

understand that who you are in a professional setting must be

a character you play. The personal version of you that is

timid or shy and the professional version must be separated

for you to become successful. Professional you must be

fearless, outgoing, and bold. Professional you must be an ass-

kicker and a fire-eater. You must wear that character as a

mask. I know that it sounds easier said than done but I can

speak from experience when I tell you that it works. The real

me is an introverted leader. I am not, naturally, an alpha

wolf. But I have studied people I want to be like enough to

create a mask for myself. I wear the mask when it is required

and put it away when it is not. You need to master the same

---

character crafting if you are a shy person. If you want to achieve, you have to act. Pissing yourself because you're too intimidated to talk to the guy who has the job you want is not going to move you closer to that goal. Challenge yourself to be more outgoing. Exercise some fortitude and if you don't think you have any fortitude, create a character that does.

You also need a way to cope with any rejection you might receive. When I was younger, rejection was crushing. It hurt to see someone else receive something I wanted so badly. However, as I got older and built up my confidence, I faced the possibility of rejection by focusing only on what I could control. My problem was never being rejected. My problem was my reaction to being rejected. I began to approach opportunities with the idea that I would absolutely be victorious. I did my best, gave a full measure of effort, and if in the end I lost, it was because the decision maker made a mistake. It was their mistake to make. I can live with it because I know I am the best choice, even when I am not rewarded for being the best choice. Be proud of your efforts regardless of the outcome.

If you can't withstand rejection, go back to the fucking basement and play video games. Mommy will bring you hot chocolate and the big, bad real world won't bother you anymore. Rejection isn't something I dealt with much until I tried moving into legitimate business. Everybody was afraid to reject me before that. But when I started moving into legitimate enterprises, I got my teeth kicked in on sales calls all day every day. Every time I spent the day getting doors slammed in my face, I wondered if I made the right choice. Every time I wondered what was wrong with me, and why it wasn't working, and how many more days of negative responses I could endure. Each time, I got up the next day and went back for more. It wasn't a mentor or spouse or friend or hypocritical life coach that pushed me to go back for more. I pushed myself. I knew I could do better. I knew those negative responses would change their minds later. I went back because I proved to myself as a tough ass little money hustling kid that I could take anything that was thrown at me. I am tougher than the big, bad real world. I took on the rejection every day and I found a way to win. You can too. If you're reading this book it's because something about me connected with something about you. You have at least a little bit of hustler in you and that little bit of hustler doesn't care about rejection. If you don't believe that, your hot chocolate is ready.

Principle 3: Be patient and Make Time

Building strong relationships takes time, as can networking to find the opportunity you want. You could spend months watching. Listening, and studying before you are finally able to make your first contact. Then each contact takes time to build a relationship with. If you're not willing to commit for as long as it takes, don't start. If you lack the fortitude to continue for as long as it takes, you'll end up resentful of the process and give up on your target. Have faith in the process and stay persistent. Remember that networking is about connection and building relationships. Even while you are waiting for the next connection, you can enjoy the connections you already have. You are using them and allowing them to use you for professional purposes, but you can still have a personal connection and enjoy knowing them as people. In the legitimate world, you're probably even safe to be friends with your connections. While you are waiting for an opportunity, keep collecting favors, strengthening relationships, and gathering intel. Don't forget to enjoy the process though. In one of my legitimate businesses, my staff started jokingly calling me the "Kingpin" because I knew everyone in town and stayed well informed on everything around me. It was always funny to me because they never knew my background or how close to on-the-nose they really were. The point is to network well, network often, and enjoy the process of being that person who just knows everybody and everything. It gives you a feeling of connection to a community that you can't get any other way. Good networking may be the cure for introversion.

While you are waiting and working your way up through your connections, get to know the company you are trying to infiltrate. My network is not just people, it is equal parts information. Stay up to date on everything happening inside the company you want to work at. Learn as many members of the management team as you can. Learn about their families, their hobbies, and their ambitions. Buy lunch for an assistant within the company but instead of asking for a job, focus on getting to know the company and management, any upcoming acquisitions, awarded contracts, and even recent firings. Know which "family" or manager runs each "territory" or department and who the final decision maker is in each. Good networking is like espionage with a positive outcome. If you are doing it well, it is like stalking but because it is a company and not a person, your stalking is called research.

All the information you gather will continue to be invaluable after you get the job. If you've already connected with someone higher in the company, ask the assistant to just mention your name or make an introduction. If they're not comfortable, don't push but most don't mind if you are genuinely friendly to them. If they do choose to make an introduction, just introduce yourself and share your ambition but don't press for an opportunity higher than entry level. Getting greedy or getting ahead of yourself will collapse an entire network. Networking is using personal relationships as currency. You need to build up your currency slowly. If you overextend yourself or spend currency you don't yet have, you'll embarrass your connections and end up bankrupt and searching for a new target to start your network all over.

Principle 4: Focus on the relationship, Not Your Resume

Since you kids don't do anything but the Internet and video games now, you don't have any damn social skills. Then, when your parents threaten to disconnect your internet to get you to leave the house, you spaz out and go door to door with your resume like you're organizing a car wash. Don't pass your resume to everyone that has hands. It's not a flyer. Don't be such a fucking "try hard". In our business, a "try hard" is either a snitch or a cretin. Neither a snitch or a cretin will ever be welcomed in business, legitimate or otherwise. Leave the resumes at home to start your network.

Truly focusing on relationships will make a more powerful impression than one more sheet of paper for them to keep track of. The Outfit doesn't accept resumes because they don't like to write down their accomplishments. To impress them you sell your reputation instead of a resume. Your deeds and relationships are all you have and there is no puffery and bullshit. You have to be a proven hard ass.

Networking is the same idea. Sell yourself first. Make friends and connections. Get to know each of them personally. Be quick to do a favor for any of them if it is within your abilities. Think of it as a game where you are trying to get them to ask you for a resume rather than you offering one. If, or when, they ask for your resume, tell them you'll have it to them on a date and time and follow through. Not having it when they ask for it creates an opportunity to show them you are organized, efficient, and professional.

Present yourself as a likable person before you try to sell your professional worth. Mutants and creeps work in retail. Nobody wants to hire the guy that gives the rest of the crew the creeps. The relationship you build is the difference between your resume being a coffee coaster or a top prospect. If you don't make the interviewer care about you, the resume is just words on a page that all look the same as the other candidates. Think of it as trying to sell a used car. You have the exact same car as everybody else to sell. That is a bleak prospect unless you paint yours red before the sales pitch. Your personal connection is the red paint. It makes you stand out from all the other plain gray cars. I've known people to network well enough that they just get the opportunity without a formal interview or presentation of a resume. They just spent so much time at the company building their relationships that they just eventually got put on the payroll and climbed from there.

Principle 5: Follow-Up

Following up accomplishes several goals for you. Investing that extra time demonstrates that you are thinking about that connection after the initial meeting. It also shows the contact you are organized, efficient, and professional. Follow-up doesn't need to be a grand gesture or grandiose display. Follow-up can be as simple as thanking a contact for meeting with you. Seriously, a simple card that says, "Thank you for your time", is all I am talking about. You can of course do more, but I would caution against going too far. Keep gestures simple. To really make the most of a follow-up, send along a small gift relevant to your conversation. Again, I want to emphasize *small*. A small token gift shows them you were listening and reinforces that you are investing in the relationship and not just using them for the connection. A large gift is ass-kissing and may compromise your contact due to company policies regarding bribes and gifts. Keep it small enough to be discrete. Just be careful what article you send. In the Outfit, these follow-up gifts have, in many cases, become nicknames. If you borrow a nickel at lunch and cleverly return the nickel with two pennies of interest as a follow up, you become Tony Nickel. This is not a bad moniker to live with. If your contact drops mustard on their shirt and you cleverly send them a stain stick as follow-up, you could become Joey the Stain. This is an unflattering moniker that will not help your reputation or garner you any respect. This is the moniker of an imbecile that sent the wrong follow-up gift after he caused his capo to drop the mustard in the first place (allegedly). The legitimate world is not so impudent but take care with your choices just in case. Nobody wants to spend a career being called Bobby Napkins or Vinny the Lugnut.

The follow-up protocol is especially true if your original contact puts you in touch with someone new. Getting the next connection given to you is a gift. It doesn't happen all the time so be sure you show respectful appreciation every time it does happen. After you reach out to the new contact, let your original contact know you've been in touch and keep them up to date on any responses. Don't give them a play by play of the details. They just need to know you did what you said you would, and it was a positive result. The follow-up shows gratitude, the update encourages them to stay vested in your success, and both of these steps together strengthen your personal relationship with that connection. It also gives assurances that you won't forget that relationship when you get what you want.

Getting What You Want

When you do finally arrive in that office, don't leave until you schedule a time to take that target to lunch. The old adage "don't take no for an answer" is the intent at this point but you can't be a pushy asshole or security will throw you, literally, out the front of the building. Understand that no doesn't really mean no in this context. No simply means, "I am not comfortable saying yes right now." There are polite, professional, respectful ways to overcome uncertainty. The easiest way to overcome uncertainty is to be prepared. Put some effort into it and prepare a list of possible responses. For example, the target could jump to the conclusion that you are asking for a job. You are going to at some point but at this time, it would be jumping to conclusions. Their response will be, "We don't have any openings right now", or sometimes targets deflect by saying, "I don't do the hiring." This is simply miscommunication easily corrected. Your prepared response could be something like, "I'm sorry to hear that, but I am actually just asking for a conversation about (the name of the company) and how I might prepare myself for an opportunity here. If you were me, who do you think I should talk to?" Continue thinking through objections and prepare answers for each objection. You need to empathize with your target. They get a dozen lazy kids a week asking them for jobs, and it is burdensome. If you had to deal with that kind of distraction, what polite excuse would you make to not talk to them? Prepare a response that is apologetic, isolates or disarms their objection, and ends in a question that is not a "yes" or "no" answer. If you screw up and ask a yes or no question, you deserve the "no" you will inevitably receive. Never ask yes or no questions, the stakes are too high to let it all your networking end with a single negative word.

Walk the fine line between persistent and pest. It is very easy to cross that line and get into trouble so try to err on the lesser side. Remember that you are judged persistent or a pest based on the standards of the target. You cannot use your own filter because you are not in a position of authority. You can try to empathize, but you don't have any idea what it is like to be in that target's position. Generally, be genuine and sincere in your request and you should be ok. Humility goes a long way too. You can build your ego later, but this is the time to be humble.

CHAPTER 2

Making "The Introductions"

Making "The Introductions"

The Networking Lunch

The Outfit is not quick to trust, and failure has a terrible consequence. Your reputation is now acceptable based on your networking or that of your sponsor on your behalf but there still must be "the introductions" before the Outfit allows you to complete any assignments on their behalf. They need assurances that you are fit and capable of accomplishing assignments. They need assurances that you are what you claim to be, and you will not be a liability to them or their profit.

The lunch or meeting you finally arranged with your target is what we call "making the introductions". Dress for that appointment like it is a communion service and prepare like it is a special operations mission. Recon, plan, and study before the appointment. Carry a pen and a cigarette lighter because your target will need one of the two during your appointment and you need to be quick to provide them even if they don't use them. Have a business card and resume available also but don't offer them until you are asked. If the target doesn't ask for them, don't give them. Don't bore your target with your resume. Resumes are for job interviews. You don't have a job interview yet. This is an opportunity to build a personal relationship with someone who could give you what you have been working for. Don't screw it up by handing them a resume. This seems counterintuitive but presenting a resume will activate their defenses and you will make the rest of the meeting more difficult for yourself. Wait until you are asked for the resume.

Remember, you're not trying to obtain a job during this lunch meeting. Focus on your personal relationship. That relationship is your goal. You need to establish a relationship that will continue after you pay the check. Keep the target bragging about themselves as much as you can. You only speak to agree with them. The more you agree with the target, the smarter they will think you are. Just don't get carried away. Nobody likes an ass-kisser. Don't disagree but make a few counter points so the target knows you can think for yourself. Just keep your counter points away from religion, politics, and family and you should be safe. Take good notes so the target knows you are listening and that you respect their experience. Tip generously so your target doesn't know how desperate you are for a decent job *and* because the wait staff is going to be one of your network connections that you asked to make sure the target's glass never dipped below half. Like I said, work every possible angle. Do not directly ask for an interview, but don't pass any opportunity to let the target know that your goal is to get an interview.

Before the end of your lunch, start asking what you can do for them next. Sort files, create some sketches, clean their Lincoln or pick up their dry cleaning. You just need them to give you a task that requires a follow-up meeting. Keep repeating the follow-up meetings until your opportunity presents itself. By the time that opportunity arrives, your target will wonder why you are interviewing because they'll think you already work there.

Resumes

In my past life, we didn't have resumes. The Outfit gets a little nervous when you start to write down their education, experience, skills, personality, and connections. There are already enough government officials doing it for them. However, in legitimate business, a quality resume is a must have to get the job you want. When writing a resume, emphasize both the quality and quantity of your past accomplishments. A little puffery is not uncalled for and is even anticipated. There are a ton of books available to tell you how to write a resume and they all do a better job than I can do. So, I will give you some tips from my perspective and let you develop your own resume.

First, understanding what is expected in your industry and position is a vital step in knowing what the best approach is to format your resume. If you want a job as a cartoonist, doodles on the page are a welcome addition to a resume. If you want a job as human resources director, you might want to stick with the text-only approach. Search online to find and review some relative industry examples.

Consider fonts carefully. I can't see as well as I used to so I always gravitate toward clean, clear san serif fonts like Calibri, Arial, and Helvetica on resumes. While you want your resume to stand out, you need it to be clear to read to be well received. Focus on aesthetically pleasing, clean fonts.

Font size needs to be around 10-12 points. The tendency for well-qualified applicants is to drop the font size so they can fit more information. That makes the page harder to see and all those qualifications go unread. Your goal is to keep your resume brief. If possible, format it to fit on one page, and it should never go longer than two. Sticking to the most relevant information makes this possible. Hiring managers briefly skim resumes for the most relevant information and having a clean, concise, relevant resume makes your continued candidacy more likely. You are always better to reduce the number of bullet points, raise the font size, and blow them away in the interview when you tell them all the stuff you left out.

While there are many ways to organize your resume, focusing on importance displays the qualities that make you the best candidate for the job. One of the best resumes I've seen showed two relative jobs under work experience and looking at the dates, there was a gap in employment which is a red flag for me. But under the second job, there was a single line that impressed me very much. It simply said, "full job history available on request. The candidate respected my time by showing me only what I needed to know and keeping the resume to a single page. I requested the full history at the interview and when it was promptly provided to me, there were no job gaps and even more experience than the candidate had included. When I look at resumes, I don't care about chronology. I care about finding and recruiting people who will make me the most profit with the least headache. Show me your prioritization skills, save me the headache, and show me why you are going to make me more money than the rest of the candidates. In a competitive workforce where employers have a lot of options, organizing by importance offers a strong focal point that will at least get you into the interview.

Finally, before you submit a resume, proofread for grammatical errors, misspellings, and typos. I have seen resumes that were so bad they should have been written in crayon. An edited resume with no mistakes will make a good impression and indicates that you are capable and pay attention to detail. Only an idiot would submit a resume with errors in it. The damn computer does all the editing for you. All you have to do is fix what the computer tells you is wrong. A resume with errors is a special kind of stupid and lazy. You have done a ton of work to get to this point. Proofread the resume.

Interviews

Your sponsor dropped your name in the right conversation. You spent months, maybe years building the perfect network. The day you walked in the building to talk to your target, you never passed a face that wasn't in your network. When you got there, you were professional and persistent, and you were successful. You got your interview. You crafted, proofread, and submitted a perfect example of all the things a powerhouse resume should be. And now, you have been rewarded with an interview for that entry-level opportunity that leads to the job you want. Congratulations, don't screw this up.

In legitimate business, an employer will tell you an interview enables them to determine if your skills, experience, and personality meet the job's requirements. They will tell you about hard skills and soft skills and cultural compatibility. Those are the official answers they have to give you about the reason they do interviews. I have completed hundreds of interviews and I'm telling you that interviews are not to select the best candidate based on anything they say or do in the interview. How could they match skills, experience, and personality to the job by asking all the candidates the same predictable questions (for which there are easily prepared answers)? Interviews are a process of elimination. Interviews are to eliminate liars, losers, idiots, and cretins. The first elimination is based on resumes. You either cleared that round by networking around it or survived that round by submitting a resume that blew the hiring manager out of their seat. Now that you are interviewing, your goal is to not screw it up. That is what interviews are truly for. You are trying to be the last candidate after the eliminations. You don't have to be the best person for the job, you just need to screw up the interview less than the other candidates. Keeping that in mind also helps calm the nerves.

For your interview, you need to be prepared. Memorize all those easily prepared answers to all the same predictable

feigned compliment. Remember, you are trying to master and maximize your ingenuity, and fortitude, and understanding of human nature. You have to take rivals out this time but don't make unnecessary enemies. If you are successful, any competent rivals will make good subordinates later. Don't make enemies unless there is profit in having them so.

After the Interview

Naturally, you got the position. The other candidates never stood a chance. They've never been hungry like you. They've never hustled like you. They didn't read this book like you.

In keeping with everything I've said thus far, show respect and loyalty to everyone as you start to achieve your goals. Send notes of thanks to any other employers you have interviewed with. Send a pleasant and professional resignation letter to the employer you are departing from. Even if it was the worst job you ever had, make no enemies unless there is a profit to be made by doing so. Give proper notice and don't burn bridges. You never know which of those you disrespected in your past might have the potential to become your ally in the future. Think of it as preserving future profit potential.

CHAPTER 3

Beginner's Rules

Beginner's Rules

Once you have the job, you need to begin planning your next move immediately. That will, of course, involve more careful observation and planning. Much like when you were building your network, you need to learn the status quo, make allies, and build your advantage so you are prepared to capitalize when your opportunity appears. I know you just got the job and you'd like to relax and just enjoy the victory for a few weeks. That's fine if you can convince your rivals to take the same few weeks off. Every minute you stop to celebrate your victory gives your rivals time to overcome their disadvantage. Now is not the time to relax. The capo wants to make sure his new hire can make him a profit. You have the momentum of your victorious interview and you know your capo is watching every move you make for at least the first six weeks. This is a select opportunity and you need to capitalize on it.

I can't advise you how to do the job well. That is something you will need to do on your own. What I can advise you on is how to avoid common new hire catastrophes. These may seem like common sense, but these are my beginner's rules to avoid disaster. While you are doing the job, applying your skills, and planning for your first promotion, follow the beginner's rules. These rules will apply every time you begin a new position, not just when you first onboard so study them well. They may well save your career.

The Beginner's Rules are simple. There are only four, but they need to be understood and followed implicitly.

Rule #1:   Keep your mouth shut. You don't know the social order. You don't know the loyalties, the back stories, or the family ties. What you don't know could fill volumes. It is all too easy to make a comment about the capo's nephew eating your lunch out of the break room fridge to someone you didn't realize was part of the family. Then the nephew makes a big humiliating show about it and plays the victim while you end up outcast. Learn and study your surroundings quietly. If you have to speak, let it be all questions. You are not listening if you are always the one talking. It has also been my experience that the smartest person in the room is usually the quietest. Talk very little and agree with other people and they will all think you are a genius. Nobody calls the person that always agrees with them stupid. You can make friends and be cordial. Just remember not to make any derogatory statements about anyone and spend most of your time listening. Just keep your mouth shut.

Rule #2:   Do what you're told. This goes without saying but I want to be crystal clear because young people now don't seem to understand what employment means. If I were hired as a Vice President of Operations at a company, I would have certain expectations about what my job duties would entail.

However, my acceptance of employment means I agree to, on a continuing basis, sell the company a certain number of hours per week in exchange for an agreed upon amount of money. As long as the company continues to meet their end of that arrangement, I report to the capo they tell me, I work on the project they assign me, and I perform whatever menial tasks they ask of me. If they want to pay me as Vice President but they tell me to clean the toilets, my paycheck will be on time and the damn toilets will be sparkling. Don't bitch about what you will or won't or don't want to do. If you are accepting their payment, do what they ask. You never know what is a test, and you don't know your capo's motivation for assigning things. Do what you are told.

Rule #3: Keep your eyes open. Your new employer will assign your primary job functions, but your secondary function should always be observation. You should have a vague idea of how the company works from your networking and interview reconnaissance. Now you need to fill in the gaps. You need to recognize every piece of the puzzle and find where they fit in the bigger picture. Be mindful of everything around you. Observe the real world and how the people in it act and react. And always tactfully take notes.

Rule #4: Keep your fly zipped. This goes for male or female hustlers. This should be a lifelong rule, not just when you are a beginner. As it was explained to me, "don't shit where you eat." Your income, your future, and your ambitions are all hinged on you maintaining your employment. Don't endanger that with office romance. Never date at or even adjacent to work. Adjacent meaning don't even date close friends of coworkers. It always ends badly. I have never seen a workplace romance that didn't end in some negative consequence. I've seen employees that thought the romance was worth the consequence, but these are an overwhelming minority of cases. Besides all those facts, you are a street hustler trying to defy the odds. People want you to fail. People want you to do something stupid. Look around your office on day one and if there isn't a coworker you would be willing to quit on day one for, then you need to avoid it later as well. Unzip your fly at your own peril.

Spend your time shaping yourself, acquiring the tools, and working to eliminate the traits you have that will hinder your next opportunity. This will be difficult through your first few steps. You are a beginner, and you don't know the culture, expectations, or procedures. If you don't slow down and figure out a complete picture of how things work, you'll be a bull in a china shop doing more damage than good. As you progress through the company via multiple promotions, your transitions will become easier and less deliberate. You will already know the basics and will only need to add new knowledge relative to your last promotion in order to prepare for your next promotion.

Ass-Kissing

I am discussing ass-kissing in this section because as a beginner or newcomer, you will be more susceptible to the practice. You will, in any business, be required to kiss a little ass. Each position you step up will reduce the required ass-kissing until you are the one extending your ring to be kissed. Until then, have the morals of a stripper and the manners of a ballerina. Ingratiation is the scientific name for ass-kissing, and it is when a staff member uses flattery, favors, and conformity to another's opinions to obtain status and preferential treatment. It is most often used with a supervisor but can also be applied with coworkers and subordinates to gain advantage or compliance. In most cases, people form more positive opinions of those sucking up to them. I still use ingratiation regularly with staff who work for me as a means of motivation. I use it because, no matter the negative connotation associated with it, whether the person is your superior or your subordinate, ass-kissing is highly effective.

However, while the person you suck up to forms a positive opinion, observers of this behavior form negative opinions and tend to dislike the ingratiator. When we see colleagues sucking up to a supervisor, we tend to dislike them or view them less favorably. Overuse of this tactic causes resentment and distrust among colleagues. Remember, just like the networking and interview process, you need to be likeable. Make no enemies unless there is profit in it.

As you start to engage with your new coworkers, you will want to be liked. Being well-liked is profitable and I would encourage you to work at being liked. However, I will caution you on using ass-kissing to gain status. Just as in networking, building a genuine personal relationship through favors and common interests is always better than a superficial relationship based on false ingratiation. When people know a behavior or statement is false or feigned, it triggers a negative reaction. Use ass-kissing to make someone feel good when they have accomplished something significant to deserve the compliment. Outside of that circumstance, ass-kissing is a dangerous path you should avoid.

If you can't resist the temptation of easy favor and you get carried away with ingratiation, you will lose allies and be seen as a doormat. Excessive ass-kissing makes people suspect your motivation and this behavior may be the kiss of death for your newly started career. That is, to be excessively polite is the ultimate rudeness. When you are fabricating complimentary statements specifically to earn a person's liking, you have gone too far. Continued disingenuous statements and behaviors deteriorate your credibility and trust further. Eventually any earned respect is lost, and you become a doormat. Nobody likes the doormat.

CHAPTER 4

Respect Your Capo

Respect Your Capo

Your network has gotten you an opportunity. Your resume has gotten you an interview. Your acumen has gotten you hired. You are making progress however, you are only an affiliate, not a member. To rise through the Outfit, you must prove yourself. You must make your bones. You must rise far enough above entry level for your capo to be vested in your future. You must earn enough profit to rise above a common street hustler and show your ability to lead a crew of your own. To reach that point where you are ritually invested in the business, you have to stand for honor, vengeance, and solidarity. You have to show your ability to do the work, slay the enemies, keep the secrets, and protect the capo.

This section is about finding a mentor, following orders, and making your capo your ally. This has nothing to do with being a capo, there will be other books for that. You are not ready to lead yet. Before you can lead, you must know how to follow. You must know how to show respect before you can earn respect. You must find a mentor to help guide and strengthen you as you prepare for your next promotion. You must earn time with your capo so that you can learn the lessons of the next level and thereby prepare yourself for leadership and your own crew.

Finding a Mentor

A mentor is someone you want to be like that is willing to hold you accountable along a track of progression that you determine with them based on your own goals. They are not your friend. They do not give you goals. They do not teach you. They are not cheerleaders. It is their job to see a better version of you and push you to become that improved version.

Mentors are disciplinarians. If you do something stupid, they will tell you that it was stupid. They also give you assignments to research or complete to help you not be so stupid in the future. When you are given an assignment by your mentor, you don't need to understand it to complete the assignment. The explanation will happen during or after the assignment so shut up and do as your mentor tells you.

Mentors create boundaries and limitations to make you better. They will give you an assignment to complete within a difficult set of parameters. It isn't supposed to be easy, and your mentor is not there to build your confidence or self-esteem. The parameters are to help you think in a new way. They are there to make you dig deeper for a solution than you realized you could. If you cannot complete an assignment within parameters, your mentor successfully exposed a weakness. Don't expect them to apologize or coddle your bruised ego. A mentor offers criticism to strengthen your weaknesses. Stop being a baby and do as your mentor tells you.

A mentor is busy running shit and earning money. If they are willing to take you on as a mentee, respect the commitment of knowledge they are making as well as the investment of time they are making for no additional up-front profit. They don't have time for politeness or diplomacy. A mentor is going to be frank, to-the-point, and brutally honest. If you can take the criticism, this greatly speeds your personal growth and saves time for you and your mentor. They will not speak to you gently or kindly. They have already accomplished their goals and they don't have to give you their time. If you are not smart enough to shut your mouth, do as your mentor tells you, and learn from their insights or if you can't handle their manner of speaking to you, don't waste their time.

It is not your mentor's job to provide words of encouragement and motivational speeches. They will be brutally honest with you. They will challenge you on your weaknesses. They are not there to help you "see the hope inside yourself." Stop being a crybaby and do as your mentor tells you

One of the reasons for mentorship is to study an experienced person who has traveled the same path you want to travel. A mentor is you cartographer. They have the map you need to get where you want to go. Navigating and maintaining corporate mobility is a high-speed run through a dark forest in the middle of the night with no moon. Your mentor knows where the quicksand is along the path. They know which wolves will help you and which ones will bite you. They know when to run fast and when to save your strength. They have night vision goggles. This section is about why you need a mentor, but can you think of a reason why you wouldn't need one?

Mentors are incredibly valuable sources of knowledge. The knowledge they have is not generic industry standards. Mentors have specialized knowledge that you will need to get you where you want to go. They have the kind of specialized knowledge that isn't on YouTube. They have the knowledge that is only available after late nights at the office, lost accounts, missed opportunities, and million-dollar mistakes. They have been through it all and they are still around to tell you about their experiences. They can dramatically shorten your learning curve if you are smart enough to learn from their experience.

Mentors know the milestones along the way. Mentors have been through similar milestones while making their bones.

Mentorship also gives you a closer look to allow you to "evaluate the fruit". The only motivation you should expect is when you are detailing your mentor's new Lincoln or picking up their dry-cleaned cashmere suits that cost more than you make in 6 months. Use these tasks and assignments to motivate you. Every moment you spend inside the life of your mentor gives you a glimpse into the future you are working so diligently to build. You might not be ready for this life yet but the more time you spend in it, the better prepared you will be for it when it does happen to you.

The other big advantage of evaluating the fruit is learning how to invest your success. You need to watch and learn how to behave and who to befriend as your wealth and assets grow along with your success. How does your mentor keep his money? What luxuries do they invest in? What investments do they stay away from? What investments does your mentor regret not making? How can you do better when you have this life for yourself? You get to see inside what you are working to become. You learn how to run your household, and how to set boundaries and budgets for yourself in your personal life. No on-the-job training will teach you how to handle your success. Only a successful mentor can provide this training.

Do you remember all those pages you read about networking? Mentors also have the ability to share their network and expand your network exponentially. They can triple your upper level connections by inviting you to a single dinner party. Those contacts are not blind contacts that you need to develop from scratch. An introduction from your mentor gives you credibility that you cannot buy or fake. You start out with a personal relationship and can move straight to strengthening that relationship and exchanging favors. And even in this task that you've done so many times before, your mentor can tell you what benefit to expect from each contact so you don't waste valuable time developing a connection who ultimately won't help you.

My most important advice regarding mentorship is don't check out when you feel challenged. Your mentor will evaluate your skills and abilities and assign you tasks to test your limits. If you fail, there is harsh feedback and if you succeed, they'll give you something more difficult next time out. There are times when you will feel bullied. There are times you will wonder what in the hell your latest assignment has to do with advancing your career. Mentorship requires strength, faith, and self-motivation. You cannot wither under pressure if you hope to benefit from a mentorship.

Mentorship is not about words of encouragement or uplifting motivational speeches. If your mentor is a kind, friendly, and encouraging person who genuinely cares about you as a person, drop them fast and find a new mentor. You are not in this to make friends. You need a mentor as ruthless and ambitious as you. It is nice to hear encouraging words and positive affirmation, but you are a street hustler. Stop being so damn needy. A mentor's job is to make you better, faster, and stronger by consistently trying to break you. Knuckle up and power through. A mentor has enough experience to see the stronger version of you if you can stop being a crybaby and respect your mentor. Mentors push. They push hard. If you are close to your limit, they push even harder. Once they understand your skills and abilities, they give you tasks of increasing difficulty and those tasks are progressively further outside your comfort zone. They find your weaknesses before your enemies. You must be smart enough to recognize what they are doing and reinforce those weaknesses before your next task. If your mentor is doing what they should, you can bet the next task is going to target that weakness and try to break you. Mentors for hustlers like us need to be ruthless. This is how they are able to find every weakness you have and then use their knowledge to improve you and turn that weakness into strength.

Your capo at the new job must follow Human Resources best practices and local labor laws. Your mentor does not. They can use whatever means necessary to improve you and prepare you to assume the mantle of leadership. Your capo and you mentor may be the same person, but you will both need to make a distinction between capo and mentor.

If your capo is your mentor, you didn't aim high enough when you selected a mentor. You want a mentor to be as high as you can get in the corporate ladder. Climbing the ladder extends your view with every rung. The better perspective a mentor has, the longer they can help guide you. Don't just pick the mentor that is easiest to obtain. In the case of mentors, never settle for the low hanging fruit. Aim for the top of the tree.

Learn to Follow

Before you can command, you must learn to follow. When a capo blows in a direction, you bend in that wind. When a capo gets hot, you stand there and sweat. In short, when you are in a subordinate position, you behave like a subordinate.

When you meet with your capo, speak when spoken to. When you speak, only add to your capo's point and never contradict them. If you have additional information to contribute, give it only if it is requested. The only exception is when the information you have is extremely vital. The phrase "extremely vital" has a different measure in our world than it does in legitimate business, but you must use your judgment just the same. If you are not spoken to, or information is not being requested, stand silent and support your capo.

Make Your Capo your Ally

"Tratta Con Quelli Che Sono Miglio De Ti E Fagli", is an Italian phrase used to describe how you should conduct yourself around your capo. It means, "Associate with those better than you and pay full expenses", roughly translated. This defines your relationship with your capo. Don't question any task your capo gives you. Undertake anything they require without thought of job description or pay grade. Capos have authority and power (both things that you want). It doesn't matter how they got it or if they deserve it - they have it. They are people with clout and if you want them to use it on your behalf do what is asked of you. Walk their dog, pay for their lunches, pick up their dry cleaning, or do whatever menial task they assign to you. If you watch and learn as I have previously instructed, none of these tasks are menial. He who cannot endure the bad will never see the good.

Respect is not reciprocal at this point in your career. Respect is an upward flow. Don't expect a pat on the back or special recognition. Your work was given to you by your capo and thereby belongs to them and you have no right to claim the credit until you are their equal. Your capo is important to your future and you must show them that you understand and appreciate that. Always show them proper respect.

Later in your career, if a capo from earlier in your career gets in the way of your own advancement, what should you do? Eliminate them, no question, they had their time and it is your time now. You are not indentured to a capo forever. When you are in a subordinate position, you behave like a subordinate. When you are no longer in a subordinate position, adjust your loyalties to reflect that fact. If you always think and act on your own behalf and you will reach the top.

If your capo is incompetent, DO NOT embarrass them or show them up. Given time, they will do that on their own.

For now, they are your capo. And when they are no longer your capo, the Outfit will need someone who shows proper respect, intelligence, cunning, and tenacity to take their place should some tragedy suddenly cause their early "retirement". Position yourself to be their replacement.

CHAPTER 5
Principles Of Business

Principles of Business

Each section thus far is about action. We have talked about what you need to do to get the job. Now you have the job, you have a mentor, and you are beginning to make the bones you need to create that next opportunity for yourself. I cannot predict each decision you will encounter along the way, but I do want to prepare you to make those decision the best way I know. As such, I want to go over some common business principles to help guide your decisions.

Honesty

Companies and corporations tell you nothing except lies. If they tell the truth, it happens by accident. They have people who specialize in burying the truth in bullshit so they can continue their lies. Some of the highest paid positions in these companies are public relations and marketing. They pay their spin doctors more than they pay their lawyers. The Outfit is no different. This thing of ours has actually combined lawyers and spin doctors. They bury bullshit and untangle legal issues.

In the legitimate business world, believe nothing and be on your guard against everything. However, the most important thing in *your* business relationships is a reputation for honesty. The companies and corporations tell nothing but lies but you have to have a reputation for honesty. Does that make sense to you? Before you get indignant about it, stop bitching and read the sentence again. The most important thing in your business relationships is a *"reputation"* for honesty. If you can genuinely fake honesty, you'll be a success, never doubt it. I have always struggled with this.

I don't fake very well. I have found that the best way to keep my reputation is silence. When I can be honest, I am. When it is a disadvantage for me to be honest, I deflect or don't respond. That is how I have coped over the years. Those that have thrived beyond my level are able to feign honestly and make people believe it. They have a natural ability to convey impure intentions through pure bullshit and make others believe in their honesty. When these people are on your side, it is fascinating to watch them use this special talent. When they are against you, it is frustrating and terrifying. If you find someone with that ability, make them an ally. If you are someone with that ability, you are your only obstacle to success.

With that understood, know who you can trust. It is not easy to decipher who you can and cannot trust. Be slow to trust but not afraid to trust. Living your life distrusting everyone will poison all your relationships. You must find a select few inner circle members to place your trust in. When you find those individuals, never lie to someone you trust. Trust is incredibly hard to build and sometimes harder to keep. Do not deliberately mislead or deceive those close and trusted few that make up your inner circle.

Integrity

Ethically, I would like to tell you to fight for your beliefs and hold tight to the courage of your convictions. However, you are still an entry-level peon. You don't have the luxury of convictions. As such, shut up and do what you are told. If you cannot prioritize your ambition over your politics and your beliefs, your corporate mobility won't take you far. Maybe you should stick to jobs with your name on your shirt where you are free to gripe and complain to your minimum wage colleagues to your heart's content. If you want to build a life of opportunity and advancement, learn to keep your convictions to yourself. Your job is to uphold your capo's and your employer's integrity, not your own.

If you want to fight for your beliefs, stand silent and stifle your objections today. Support your capo and their conviction, whether you agree or disagree, until you surpass them. Work hard, follow the strategies in this guidebook, take your opportunities, and advance yourself in the organization. When you become capo, you can afford convictions. As capo, you will then have a crew that upholds your convictions just as you do for your capo today. Until you advance to capo, you are not paid for your convictions. Learn to set personal feelings aside. Take your ego out of it and do what you are told.

Keeping Your Word

This is a critical principle in any business, legitimate or otherwise. Keep your damn word. Do what you say you will and do it the way you said you would. All the way down to repaying a quarter borrowed for the vending machine in a timely manner. You do exactly what you say you will do. Breaking your word is a slippery slope. You pay back the quarter one day late. Then you repay a few dollars late. Then you think you can wait an extra week before you pay that bill that is due. Each time you break your word, you are convincing yourself that it is acceptable. You are slowly justifying the behavior to yourself and you will inevitably escalate the behavior if nobody holds you accountable. Today it is just a quarter you paid back a single day late. The problem is when you allow the pattern to escalate. Just pay back the quarter on time. Keep your word and don't be a dolt.

With customers, keep the intent of your word and forget the fine print. Too many businesses convince customers to sign papers which are not explained to them properly. When mistakes happen, there is fine print entitling the company to keep the money and not correct whatever mistake was made. Over time, employees learn to exploit the fine print and feel entitled to take shortcuts due to that fine print. Don't cheat a customer or shortchange the value they were expecting, then use some unrealistic technical bullshit in order to rationalize being an asshole. There is no technical justification for breaking the intent of your word in any business. Deliver intent and forget the fine print if you want satisfied customers.

Keeping your word also includes keeping your word to yourself. Too many people don't consider the ramifications of breaking their word to themselves. If you tell yourself you will wake up an hour early for the next two weeks, then only follow through for three days, you are breaking your word. This is the same slope as repaying the quarter. You create a pattern of breaking your word to yourself and you subconsciously devalue your own word. By that subconscious justification, you begin to stop keeping your word to others as the pattern escalates. You are presumably reading this book because you want to advance in your career. In leadership, you can only hold others to the same standard you hold yourself to. You set the example and create the culture. If you expect others to keep your word to others, they need to see you keeping your word, including keeping your word to yourself. If your goal is leadership, don't wait until you are a leader to practice the required skills. Keep your word always so that is your reputation as you escalate your standing in the organization.You will have less work later to establish your expectations. Always keep your word, even to yourself.

Breaking your word to yourself or others is cowardly, no matter how you spin it. Have the courage to follow through on the commitments you make to other people. It shows the measure of your character and it shows people you can be trusted and relied on. I have kept my word through seething hatred because no matter how much I disliked who benefitted, *I* gave my word. Whatever bad behavior caused my negative feelings is not an excuse for me to behave badly. I keep my word, period. I may be a criminal, but I am not a coward. Keep your damn word.

Loyalty

Devotion to duty, friendship, and loyalty to the Outfit is easy when times are good. It doesn't take much to refuse compromising requests. Who will you be when times are less predictable? Do you have the fortitude to maintain your loyalty and avoid negative influences and conflicts of interest when the bad times come? Loyalty is about strength. If times get lean and sacrifices are being made by an entire organization to survive, you must have the mental strength to avoid temptation and to resist what you cannot avoid. If you allow weakness and temptation to surround you when your guard is down, you can't escape it when you need to. Temptation is a very tangled influence. I have seen very bad things happen to people that allowed temptation to envelope them.

Loyalty is about deciding who you are and being true to that decision at all times. Keeping friends within another rival organization when times are good may seem harmless but when conditions inevitably change, that friendship becomes compromised loyalty. Even if you have the ability to stay loyal, that connection calls your trust into question. Don't create questionable connections and conflicts of interest. Not making connections will be seen as being competitive during good times and you can make that work in your favor. Getting a phone call from a rival company that is competing for the same contract that may make or break your company cannot work in your favor. You will need to use your judgement when making outside connections. Your organization's culture may tolerate or even encourage connecting with industry colleagues. The Outfit did not have that culture, so I remain guarded with my loyalty to this day. Just make sure any connections you make will profit your company and not endanger it. Questioned loyalty is difficult to overcome.

Loyalty is also about safeguarding secrets. In the Outfit, there are not many opportunities to go work for a different organization. We don't have lateral transfers and promotional opportunities. You move up within the Outfit or you "retire". However, in legitimate businesses you will have this opportunity. If you choose to transition to another employer, keeping the secrets and maintaining loyalty through a legitimate transition to another company is about

providing a reasonable notice before you leave and

respecting the proprietary information of your soon-

to-be former employer. Keep your mouth shut and

don't act like a fucking rat. When you arrive at the

new company, don't trust anybody that asks you to

reveal proprietary information. It is usually a good

indication that you were unfairly recruited as a spy

rather than a legitimate respected employee.

Fairness

In legitimate business, fairness is not exercising

power arbitrarily, equal treatment of individuals, a

willingness to admit mistakes, commitment to justice,

and a bunch of other hippie bullshit. The business of

the Outfit is business. It is about profit. You can only

tolerate a limited amount of fairness within your

mandatory profit margins. At the end of the day,

fairness is the hustler with the best preparation,

knowledge, work ethic, and network making the most profit. If that hustler had time to sabotage three other people and still make more profit than the three of them, that isn't unfairness to those three. That is a resourceful hustler doing what needs to be done.

Fairness, in many cases, is also about not taking undue advantage of another's mistakes. However, for a street hustler, their mistake is a fair advantage. If you find an advantage, squeeze all the profit you can from it. Take your opportunity. Fairness is equality. If the 'screw-up' is your equal, when he makes the mistake, fairness is not treating him like the idiot he is as you take full advantage of your opportunity. If you pass up an opportunity like this, you will never make your bones. That idiot had the same opportunity to be ruthless and he shit the bed. Capitalize on the mistake and don't you dare feel guilty about it.

What does fairness have to do with business anyway? You need to put fairness out of your head. The entire industrial revolution is littered with men who committed ruthless acts that would land a modern executive in prison. Henry Ford, Thomas Edison, William Randolph Hearst, Ray Kroc, and countless others are remembered as the men who built this country into a world superpower. They were also opportunists who took every unfair advantage to crush upcoming competition under their boot heel. Ford maliciously drove his investors out because he saw them as parasites despite his not contributing any of his own cash to start the company. Edison ran a national smear campaign when Tesla invented a superior electrical transmission system. He even convinced the federal government to revoke some of Tesla's patents. Hearst used his money to start wars in third world countries in order for his newspaper empire to have something interesting to print in the headlines. Ray Kroc manipulated the McDonald's company right out from under the McDonald brothers leaving them only the original location with a court-ordered name change. After which, Ray opened a brand-new McDonald's across the street and crushed the original location out of business. Fairness is not what builds success. Opportunity builds success and you need to be ruthless enough to seize yours no matter how fair or unfair it may be interpreted.

On my way up, I had a capo explain to me that fairness is everyone getting the same amount of ice in life. He further explained that poor people get their ice in the winter and rich people get it in the summer. Stop bitching about what isn't fair. If your ice was given to you in winter, figure out how to sell it or how to save it until summer. Industrious will win you profit, not fairness. Unfairness is something lazy people use to justify not making more of their life.

Listen and learn, tolerate, survive, lie low, and remember that your best weapon against unfairness is patience. In the meanwhile, keep your mouth shut, reinforce alliances, and do your job with a smile like a good soldier and stop worrying about fairness. There is no room for fairness in business.

Respect

There are two types of respect that need to be mentioned here. The first important type of respect is about autonomy and privacy. You should always be watching, learning, and remembering. However, you didn't see anything. You never repeat what you've seen or acknowledge that you've seen it. Respect is silence. Your silence shows respect to all those who came before you, all those who are giving you your current opportunity, and all those who will come after you. You respect your company by your silence. Keep silent unless it is for strategic advantage or substantial profit. However, for your current status and position, those decisions are still above your head, peon. For now, keep your mouth shut.

The second type of respect is accepting your position and showing proper gratitude to those that gave it to you. Don't speak out of turn. Don't "show up" your capo. Never communicate outside the chain of command. This respect flows up through the organization but not always down. A good capo will respect their crew, but they don't have to and you shouldn't expect them to. That doesn't make them mean or rude. It makes them effective. There are ways to be polite and respectful, but you are not in a position to pass judgement on your capo's management choices. Remember, you are still learning to follow. Watch, learn, shut up, never refuse an assignment, nothing is beneath you, and you always buy your capo's lunch. When you are making your bones, this is proper respect.

Accountability

While accountability in legitimate business is critically important, it has a much darker tone in my business. In either business world, hold yourself accountable. If your capo asks you to deliver five accounts, your goal needs to be six. Set your own goals higher so that in pursuit of your goals you are able to accomplish the goals of your capo even if you fail to reach your own goal. You always need to hold yourself to a higher standard. If you don't, someone else will.

In legitimate business, accountability is not about trying to "catch" employees doing something wrong, ratting out coworkers, or laying down a strict set of rules administered with a punitive approach.

Accountability is about setting and holding people to

a common standard by clearly defining the expectation and establishing a measured consequence for any failure to meet the expectation. Accountability is performance evaluations at scheduled intervals and a standardized structure to review performance based on key performance indicators that the employee is made aware of before and during the evaluation period. Accountability is making an employee fix their own mistakes over and over, rather than just having an employee that is better at the task redo the mistakes. Employee accountability means holding all levels of employees responsible for results of their choices and results. And if you think your capo is a ball-buster for holding you accountable by these means, keep in mind that in my former life accountability could include being bashed with a bag full of nickels.

CHAPTER 6
Time Management

Time Management

Every job, both legitimate and otherwise, has "waiting around" time. Make your waiting around time pay for itself. Read or study something. Every business has plenty of ambitious, lazy people. Your colleagues will spend their time bullshitting, playing cards, and surfing useless videos about nonsense. They gossip around the water cooler, the coffee machine, the copy machine, or the break room. You are a hustler, don't lose sight of where you came from when it looks like you're going to get where you're going. Hustlers stay working. You can skip the gossip and nonsense. Courtesy requires that you bullshit with your peers on rare occasion, and you will need to maintain a minimum of association with your peers. However, keep it to the minimum. If you spend too much time with them, human nature is for you to inevitably fall into their patterns. Associate enough to be friendly but keep enough distance to maintain your own habits. Find productive work for your spare time that attracts good notice, fills your pocket, reinforces power, or makes your capo look like a superstar. Spending your "waiting around time" on anything that doesn't accomplish one of those things is laziness. Find a sideline activity for yourself. I have written most of this book on small devices like a phone or tablet. These words are a result of my "waiting around" time. What can you do in your wasted moments over just a few months with new habits?

If you have the ability, choose the time of day or night when your energies are highest and conduct your business at that time if it can be arranged. Obviously, this will be more difficult to arrange in a legitimate business. If your chosen career allows flexible hours, do business when you are at your best, not when your adversaries are at theirs. If you do have to do something at an inconvenient time for you, show up just long enough to reschedule. The best thing to invest in your business or career is your time. To schedule, plan, and use time effectively, know your objective, opportunities, and obstacles then devise your strategies.

Your best and most effective strategy for time management is delegating. Delegating is to send or authorize someone else to do something as a representative of you. The person you delegate a task to does not have to be a subordinate. If coworkers are better at certain tasks or enjoy them more than you, trade off and let them do that task. If another department would rather complete part of a task after you transfer the task to them, let them do that task. If some ambitious networking hustler wants to come in on a Saturday and complete some menial task in exchange for some experience, let them do that task. Get others to do as much as you can for you. As a rule, you should follow these three basic rules of effective time management:

Rule #1:   Schedule your tasks

Rule #2:   Delegate them.

Rule #3:   Delegate more of them.

position shows immediately that you are above average and that you are willing to be held accountable. You may be held accountable for a few mistakes but you will also reap the rewards of the victories.

Leadership

Making decisions shows leadership ability. Leadership is the action of leading a group of people or an organization. The important word in that definition is "action". When a decision needs to be made, take action. Step forward and embrace the responsibility. Make a decision and your coworkers will usually follow. By making a decision that your coworkers endorse and follow, you are demonstrating the ability to lead others. You are also providing yourself an example of leadership to be used in later advancement interviews, so be sure to write it down.

Reasoning

Decision making is a reflection of your reasoning ability. In order to make decisions, you have to look at multiple possibilities, evaluate the positive and negative aspects of each option and use your reason to decide. Careful decisions made by reasoning are a necessary skill for leaders.

Intuition - Intuition is what you know based on instinct rather than reasoning. Reasoning is conscious and intuition is subconscious. Making decisions carefully by reasoning is not always an option for leaders. Performing the process under pressure shows your superiors the quality of your intuition.

Creativity

The last quality that decision making will reveal to your superiors is your creativity. Many times, the decision is unclear or needs to be a combination of multiple options. These decisions give you opportunities to flex your creativity. Of the qualities on this short list, creativity is perhaps the rarest ability and also the most valuable. I am good at reasoning and intuition, but I am great at creativity and I would strongly encourage you to develop your ability to be creative and devise solutions from original ideas.

Effective time management is making sure you have less time you have to work. Maximize your "waiting around" time. This keeps everyone around you too busy to maneuver for the next promotion and allows you plenty of "waiting around" time to learn new skills, kiss a little ass, and network your way into an opportunity. Make certain you have hours every day, then days every week, then weeks every year to dedicate to "waiting around" time endeavors. The truest objective of time management should be to not work. Work smart, not hard. Time management is not creating a twenty-fifth hour, it's handling your business in 6 hours or less, and those not every day.

You must know your objectives. Once you do, assess the obstacles and opportunities, devise strategy and tactics, manage your resources and risks, and decide who does what in what sequence. That is all you need to do. You move the pieces on the board.

It would be easy to say this is your capo's responsibility. However, managing those around you, keeping your peers on task, and engineering yourself a better use of your time can be done at every level of an organization and is noticed as a great quality because it is rare to find. Show yourself to have leadership abilities long before you ask to become a leader. The free time you engineer also gives you ample opportunity to make sure your superiors notice your time management skills.

CHAPTER 7
Making Decisions

Making Decisions

Decision making is an important skill for an entry level associate. Your superiors need to know you can be decisive and that those decisions demonstrate the skills required to advance. Quality decisions show you superiors the following qualities:

Problem-Solving Ability

Decisions are made in order to solve problems. Making quality decisions under pressure and/or imposing deadlines shows your ability to solve problems. It seems strange to say that it is rare to find an ambitious employee willing to solve a problem but that is precisely what I am saying. A majority of people believe solving problems is an executive's responsibility. No matter what level they advance to, human nature is for people to believe that problem solving is above their current level because they don't want to be held accountable for mistakes. To solve problems in an entry-level

Understanding the qualities that decision making will highlight will not make decisions easier. It only explains what is at stake and why you should take every opportunity to be a decision maker. In order to make decisions, you need to understand the process involved. Making decisions is a simple 7-step process and you will need to go through this process in every decision. There are times you will have to go through these steps in just moments while other times will allow you to work through the process over weeks. No matter what your timeline is for the decision, you will follow these seven steps:

Step #1: Identify the problem. This is a little more convoluted in my world than yours but be sure you correctly identify the problem. Solving the wrong problem will frustrate you and disappoint your superiors. Making decisions is about impressing them so be sure you are clear on what the problem is. I would also remind you that almost all problems are people. If your problem isn't a person or people, you are likely solving the wrong problem. The few instances that the problem isn't people, the problems are much easier to solve, and you can easily delegate those decisions. Solving the people related problems are much more difficult so take your time and solve them yourself. They are riskier problems but bring greater rewards for their solution.

Step #2:   Gather the facts. Get as much as you can of the best information possible and review it carefully. This is difficult on decisions that rely on intuition but these decisions also bring the greatest praise and reward so don't shy away when it gets difficult. Be careful of information sources as well. Many a young hustler have been undone by misinformation given maliciously by ambitious colleagues.

Step #3:   Pose solutions. Always create multiple solutions. Brainstorm and don't throw any ideas away until you have vetted their value thoroughly. The best solution is generally a combination between multiple solutions that wouldn't have been thought of had the first solution been pursued or if the unlikely ideas had been thrown away. Even bad ideas serve a purpose in this process so use your creativity and consider lots of possible solutions.

Step #4:   Foresee consequences. Draw up worst-case scenarios. Stretch your paranoia on this step. Even the most unlikely possibilities should be considered. Create pro and con lists to help you. Do whatever you need to do within the time allowed to try to foresee every possible likely and unlikely consequence of your decision. Be thorough and include the "way out" possibilities. Many of my decisions are made by figuring out that one decision's worst case is less costly than the other decision's worst case. Both outcomes were bad, so my decision came down to minimizing the consequences. Your ability to foresee consequences and mitigate or minimize them demonstrates understanding of the situation, knowledge of the company, and strong leadership ability.

Step #5: Consult your mentor. That is why you have one. You trust them and they have more experience than you. If you have the time to go through this step, you would be stupid not to ask. Your mentor has likely made the same or similar decision in the past. They may not tell you the right answer, but they will at least tell you some of the wrong answers. In multiple choice, eliminating choices improves your odds greatly. Your mentor can do the same thing for your decision making. You just have to take the time to ask them.

Step #6: Take time away from the problem. Stop thinking about it all together if you can. Do some simple repetitive or physical task that distracts you from the decision. If you have time, sleep on the decision. Let your brain sort and cross reference all the information you gathered. Through all your considering and researching and list making, your brain has been taking information into short-term memory. Getting some sleep or doing some low-brain-function tasks allows your brain to sort all that information into long-term memory so it is available to make your decision. As your brain sorts information, just like a computer maintains a database, it makes connections between similar things. As your brain sorts, it makes connections that you might not make while you are awake or actively thinking about it. Those connections often reveal pitfalls associated with a decision that you would not see otherwise. Take the time to process and connect before you decide.

Step #7:   Make your decision. Do what your gut tells you. It sounds trivial to go with your gut after you've gone through six other painstaking steps to make an informed decision but that is exactly what you should do. All the information you have prepared, gathered, and processed is now stored in your brain and your brain has drawn all the links it can find among that information. Often your "gut" will tell you that a decision is wrong. That is not some mystical psychic ability made by magic. It is your subconscious telling you something is wrong with that choice based on something your conscious hasn't seen yet. Listen to your gut. The person with the great gut will rise to the top in any business. And, the more decisions you make, the better and faster your gut will get.

Follow this process for all major decisions and look back only to evaluate results and garner knowledge for future use. The more knowledge and experience you commit to memory, the better your gut instincts will become. The better your gut, the higher your value to the organization. If you follow the seven steps, you continuously improve your gut reactions, and if you still somehow make a bad decision, do what people in every business, legitimate or otherwise, have

always done. Blame the failure on the closest disposable

cretin.

CHAPTER 8
The Water Cooler

The Water Cooler

Everybody within an organization knows what their water cooler is. The water cooler is where the know-nothing, be-nothing, malcontents go to criticize and judge those around them. In terms young people will understand, it is like social media in real life. It is rarely a literal water cooler anymore. It is a break room, coffee machine, smoking area, loading dock, or hallway where judgmental, shit-talking cowards gather to talk about other people with like-minded idiots and rats.

Surviving the water cooler is not about participating. It is about finding out who is who and what is what, and storing all this information for your own future use. Much like building your gut for decision making, you build your awareness of the political environment within the company to help you navigate the nonsensical bullshit that happens every day. Don't participate in any of the nonsense but be sure you always know what the trending nonsense is and how it works to your advantage.

Be patient, watch, listen, say little, and be patient. You didn't read it wrong, and it isn't a typo. Patience is critically important in office politicking. Reacting immediately to any of the current gossip is never the correct solution. No matter how you feel personally about what you hear, you need to carefully consider your reaction. You need to use the seven-step process from the previous chapter and consider all the possible consequences for each possible reaction. I have had instances of office politicking nonsense that worked in my favor. The gossip worked in my favor by contributing to a reputation I wanted to have. That rumor contributed to the reputation that moved me from associate to lieutenant. The smartest reaction was no reaction. I would never have arrived at that positive outcome if I had not taken the time to consider the possibilities and consequences of each possible reaction.

Rumors and subversive talk will always exist. To speak of rumors as if survival depended on them may seem extreme to you, but it shouldn't. There is always at least one coworker trying to cause you misfortune. Always, no exceptions. Do not participate in any of the rumors but be sure you always know what they are and who they are focused on. If you don't know the rumors, you can't use them to your advantage. Saving a coworker who is the victim of rumors can help you later. Knowing who is being targeted can allow you to distance yourself from any fallout. However, don't decide on your level of involvement until you answer to yourself, "What's in it for me?" and, "What's in it for them?" Use the seven-step decision making process to answer these questions and examine possible reactions. Until you have definite answers, be cordial to all and don't stand out. The obvious exception is when you are the subject of a rumor. In this case, the questions are, "Who started it?", "Why did they start it?" and "How do I eliminate it?" In most cases, having the answers to the first two questions is usually the answer to the third question and often provides a more permanent solution than fighting within the rumor mill itself. Let the who and why leak to your superiors. Do not tell them yourself but arrange for the information to arrive in front of them. If you are asked about the rumor, simply explain that you choose not to participate in office gossip, you are just trying to do a job for the betterment of the company, but you would appreciate if it could be prevented in the future. You shouldn't have to successfully execute this maneuver more than twice and the rumor mill will learn to steer clear of you. People who start these rumors are cowardly and it only takes one or two instances of them getting caught and remanded for them to learn what you are capable of. By handling the rumors in this manner, you leave an incredible impression on your superiors and thereby are better off than if the rumor had never started.

CHAPTER 9
Business Relationships

Business Relationships

Friends

Business is not the place to make friends. You can be friendly but do not make friends. Making friends in business inevitably ends in, "It's not personal, it's just business." Many friendships have ended with the utterance of this phrase. Former friends use it every day to validate their disloyal acts. Friends betray you eventually and then tell you to your face, "it's just business." That phrase will never justify stabbing a friend in the back for your own advantage and it will always be taken personally. The only sure way to not be told or be the one telling this phrase is to heed my advice and keep your friendships outside of work.

You might argue that you have a true friend. You have a friend that can be trusted. You can argue that I am wrong and untrusting and paranoid. You can choose to ignore my perspective on friends. However, the truth is that you can never know how true a friend is until they are tested. So long as things go well for you, I would argue that the required test will never come. Without a definitive test, you must assume the worst. You must acknowledge that your friend could betray you if presented the right opportunity. Otherwise, you will only find out you were wrong after it is too late to prevent. With the possibility of betrayal assumed, act accordingly. Never place absolute trust in another person. You cannot have friends, only interests.

Never tell friends how good you are doing. They either won't believe you or they'll call you a braggart and talk shit about you. Likewise, never tell friends how bad things are going. They will either gloat or they will leak word back to your enemies that you are weak. I know, you have the one friend in the wide world that is the exception (sarcasm intended) but your enemies are clever, and your exceptional friend doesn't always realize they are compromising you. You cannot have friends in business.

You don't need friends, you need allies. You don't even necessarily need to like your allies. They need to have common objectives or adversaries and be willing to share resources and information. If you want a true friend, buy a dog. Then cut the dog's tongue out just to be safe. That is the only friend you can trust in business.

Enemies

Fear your enemies. To not fear your enemy is to invite your downfall. Don't let that fear cloud your vision or make you paranoid but maintain a healthy fear. You may look around yourself and think I am exaggerating but a man without enemies is a man without qualities. If you are aware of your potential enough to read this book, you have enemies. Find out who they are as soon as possible.

Look for enemies in unexpected places. They will be among your friends, they will be among your family, they will be in your bed, and they will even be within yourself. Stay vigilant and shine a light on them when and where you find them. When you shine that light, don't watch your known enemy. Watch the eyes of others as you reveal your enemy. Enemies seldom work alone and revealing one is the best time to uncover others.

Always think the worst of your enemies and you will seldom be mistaken. But one good thing about an avowed enemy is that you know them. Once they are identified, they are somewhat predictable. You don't have to keep exerting yourself to find them. You can predict that they will make selfish and opposing decisions to yours. Predictable enemies are entertaining because they are easy to ensnare.

If you move against an enemy, be sure they are destroyed quickly and thoroughly. A wounded enemy starts plotting revenge immediately and the wound motivates them. A wound inflicted by a once defeated enemy is a difficult wound to heal. Knowing that the wound was preventable makes the pain of it exponentially worse. Finish your enemies to the point that they cannot or will not return for revenge ever. Unfinished enemies take too much energy to monitor. You need to be focused on more important things than a loose end you didn't or couldn't wrap up.

CONCLUSION

Conclusion

At this point you should be prepared to build your reputation by networking and trading in favors. Once you can exploit those connections to get to your target, you know how to survive and conquer the interview and obtain the entry-level job you need to start building your empire. I also gave you the beginner's rules, so you know how to blend in and when to stand out. You know how much to kiss ass without becoming a doormat. I explained how to show your new capo proper respect and how to interact with a mentor. We talked about principles of business and several other entry-level skills you need to master to make the correct impressions on your superiors and begin working your way up the corporate ladder. Your success story is underway. Just remember, to survive you must always be planning your next opportunity and when that opportunity materializes, you must strike swiftly. To become a capo, one attitude alone is necessary. You prepare, you study, and you watch vigilantly for an opportunity for yourself. If that means "cutting someone else's throat", that is exactly what you do. You act quickly and take what you have so patiently earned.

Now I am not going to end this book until I tell you about the rest of the *Making Bones Series* but first, I want to share a story:

There was once a church in the old country where the priest had come to an age where he felt his flock needed a younger leader. He announced at Sunday mass that he would be leaving and introduced his replacement. To his surprise, the church was jubilant and congratulated the priest on his retirement and welcomed the young priest into the church. The next week, the young priest got up and gave a beautiful mass and all the church goers were happy and thankful. On the second week, the young priest got up and gave the exact same beautiful mass and all the church goers were confused. However, they gave the new priest a break, thinking maybe he just got busy with all the adjustments to his new position.

On the third week, the young priest got up and gave the exact same beautiful mass and all the church goers called a secret meeting. They wanted to give the new priest a fair opportunity, but they didn't feel they could allow the young priest to continue repeating his sermon. It was decided that if the priest repeated the sermon again, he would have to answer for it. On the fourth week, the young priest got up and gave the exact same beautiful mass and all the church goers were outraged. They politely waited for the end of mass but when they were dismissed, nobody moved. They all stayed perfectly still until the priest returned to the pulpit. When the head of the deacons stood and asked the young priest about the repetitious sermon, the priest answered, "when you learn to apply this sermon correctly, I'll write a new one."

My point is that while I am going to tell you about the *Making Bones Series*, I will also encourage you to make sure you are properly applying the lessons in the first book before you start into the second and third books.

I caution so because in Book 2, *Rise of a Capo*, the knowledge and wisdom are intended for those who have been promoted into a leadership role, and in Book 3, *Wisdom of an Underboss*, the lessons are intended for executive level positions with multiple capos subordinate to you. As you move up through an organization, your perspective will need to change. As a result, some of the lessons in the other books are slightly different than what has been explained in *The Street Hustler's Guidebook*. Don't rush through the series. Take your time with each one and master the lessons before you move on to the next books.

When the time undoubtedly comes, make sure you check out the rest of the *Making Bones Series*!!!

OTHER BOOKS BY MOJO

Book 2: *Rise of a Capo*
As you advanced your standing using the wisdom in *The Street Hustler's Guidebook*, you collected your rewards. Now you must learn to protect them, defend them, and improve upon them. The knowledge and wisdom within *Rise of a Capo* is intended for those who have been newly promoted into a leadership role. The lessons in *Rise of a Capo* will guide you through your transition into leadership as well as skills necessary to recruit and manage your crew.

Book 3: *Wisdom of an Underboss*
You have proven your ability to lead using the wisdom within *Rise of a Capo* and have become a boss of bosses. *Wisdom from an Underboss* is filled with lessons for executive level management overseeing larger work forces while continuing to command the respect you have earned.